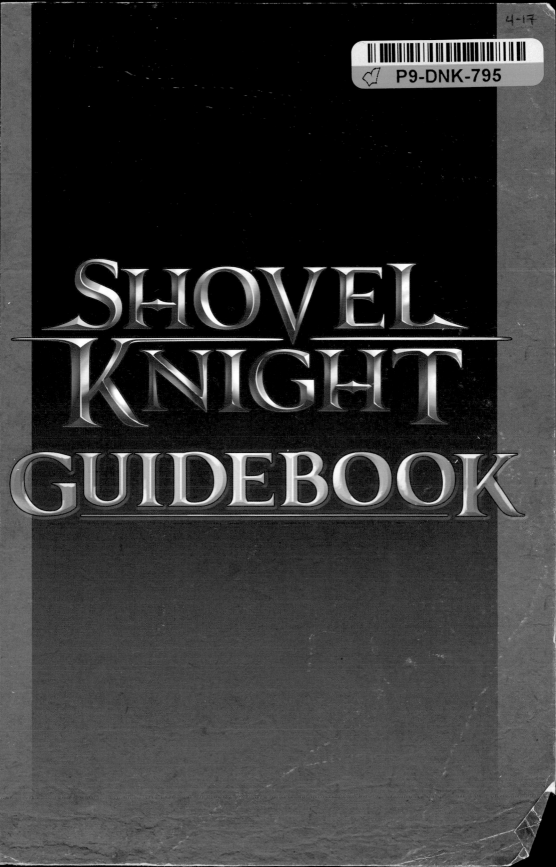

SHOVEL KNIGHT
GUIDEBOOK

GROSSET & DUNLAP
Penguin Young Readers Group
An Imprint of Penguin Random House LLC

Penguin supports copyright. Copyright fuels creativity, encourages
diverse voices, promotes free speech, and creates a vibrant culture.
Thank you for buying an authorized edition of this book and for complying
with copyright laws by not reproducing, scanning, or distributing any part of
it in any form without permission. You are supporting writers and allowing
Penguin to continue to publish books for every reader.

YACHT CLUB
GAMES

Shovel Knight is a trademark of Yacht Club Games.
© 2017 Yacht Club Games L.L.C. All rights reserved. Published by
Grosset & Dunlap, an imprint of Penguin Random House LLC,
345 Hudson Street, New York, New York 10014. GROSSET & DUNLAP
is a trademark of Penguin Random House LLC.
Manufactured in China.

ISBN 9781101996010   10 9 8 7 6 5 4 3 2 1

SHOVEL KNIGHT

GUIDEBOOK

by Lloyd Cordill

Grosset & Dunlap
An Imprint of Penguin Random House

Table of Contents

The Twelve Main Stages

The Twelve Main Stages

GREETINGS, TRAVELERS. COME CLOSER, CLEAN OUT YOUR EARS, AND I WILL TELL YOU THE TALE OF SHOVEL KNIGHT, THE GREATEST HERO AND TREASURE SEEKER IN THE REALM!

ENTER THIS DANGEROUS VALLEY, IF YOU DARE. HERE YOU MUST FACE THE ORDER OF NO QUARTER, EIGHT KNIGHTS WHO HAVE SWORN THEIR ALLEGIANCE TO THE ENCHANTRESS, A COLD AND CALCULATING FORCE OF GREAT MAGICAL POWER! SO GRAB YOUR SHOVEL BLADE AND FOLLOW ME, THE HUMBLE BARD, AS WE JOURNEY INTO THE WORLD OF SHOVEL KNIGHT!

1. Plains

A lush green land of rolling hills, grassy knolls, and leafy forests.

2. Pridemoor Keep

A bit run down until King Knight usurped the throne and gilded it with resources from the Enchantress.

3. The Lich Yard

This run-down town was this peaceful village until it became overrun with ghosts and unceasing darkness.

4. Explodatorium

If mad science and detonations are giving you problems, this alchemical lab is the source of your troubles.

5. Iron Whale

This enormous submarine is filled with booby traps to protect ill-gotten gains greedily hoarded by Treasure Knight.

6. Lost City

A long-forgotten underground metropolis, the Lost City has bubbled to the surface.

7. Clockwork Tower

An automated clockwork tower: its gear-filled halls are as dangerous as its enemies.

8. Stranded Ship

This forgotten ship, neglected and derelict, is at the mercy of Polar Knight and his invading forces.

9. Flying Machine

Captained by the carefree Propeller Knight, this level is a dangerous aerial adventure.

10. Tower of Fate (Three Stages)

The Tower of Fate is a beacon of arcane energy and lair of the wicked Enchantress.

PLAINS

Description

The valley is a land of beauty and untold riches. Nowhere is this better on display than in the Plains. Rolling hills, forests, twisting caves to explore—the Plains has it all. The halcyon days of yore ended when the Enchantress came to power. The Beetos and Dozedrakes have been hostile of late, attacking travelers and hoarding treasure.

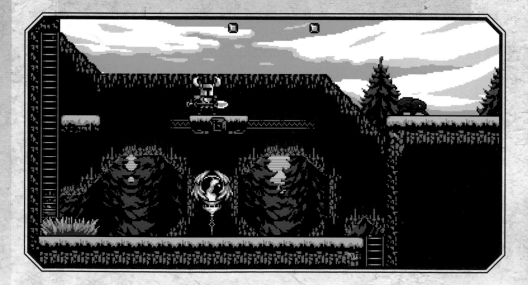

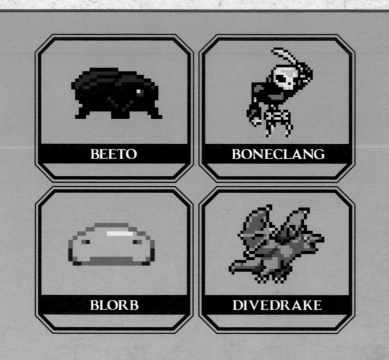

BEETO

BONECLANG

BLORB

DIVEDRAKE

Obstacles

MOUND OF DIRT

LADDER

Swing your shovel and scoop up riches when you see these piles of black dirt.

When in front of a ladder, press up or down to grab on. You can move up and down and even attack! Press jump while on the ladder to drop off.

Dozedrake

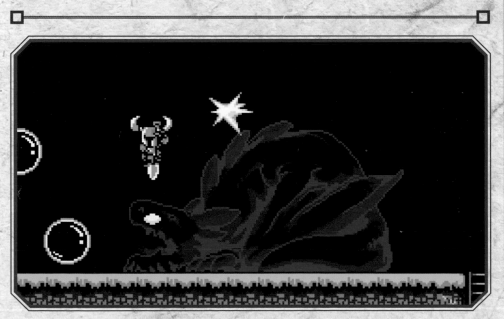

These sleeping dragons like to live in the caves of the Plains. Their heads are their weak points, and you can avoid their blasts of bubbles by Shovel Dropping onto their heads repeatedly. (To Shovel Drop, press the down button while mid-jump.)

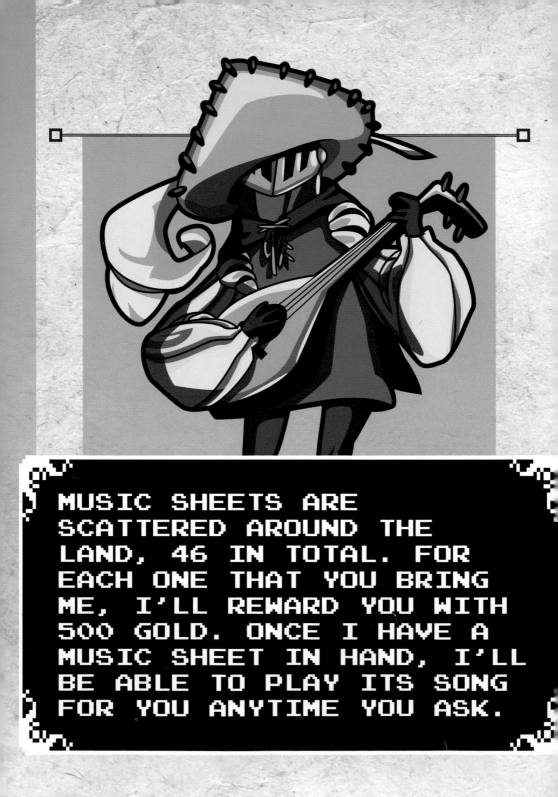

MUSIC SHEETS ARE SCATTERED AROUND THE LAND, 46 IN TOTAL. FOR EACH ONE THAT YOU BRING ME, I'LL REWARD YOU WITH 500 GOLD. ONCE I HAVE A MUSIC SHEET IN HAND, I'LL BE ABLE TO PLAY ITS SONG FOR YOU ANYTIME YOU ASK.

Music Sheet #20
Strike the Earth

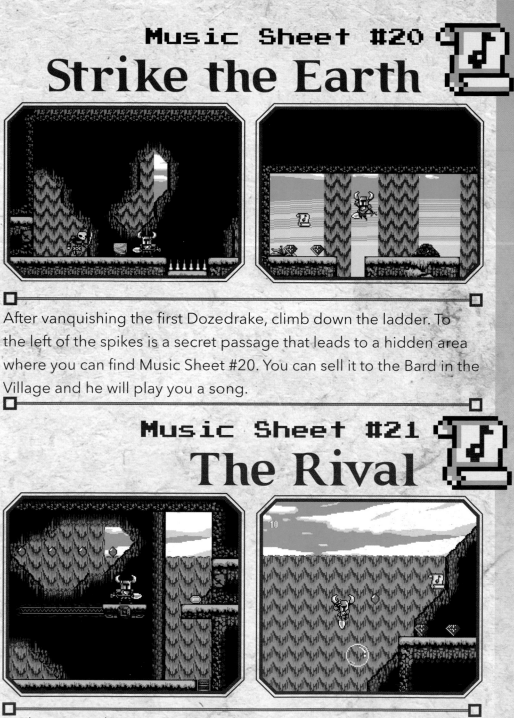

After vanquishing the first Dozedrake, climb down the ladder. To the left of the spikes is a secret passage that leads to a hidden area where you can find Music Sheet #20. You can sell it to the Bard in the Village and he will play you a song.

Music Sheet #21
The Rival

The area with two moving platforms has a secret passage on the right side. You'll have to Shovel Drop over some bubbles to reach Music Sheet #21.

Boss
Black Knight

Who is Black Knight? Though his identity is shrouded in mystery, Black Knight has been a foil to Shovel Knight for a long time. He refuses to join the Order of No Quarter, for reasons unknown.

Black Knight has been trained in the art of the Shovel Blade much like Shovel Knight has. He can jump high into the air and drop down on top of you with a Shovel Drop of his own. He has some other tricks up his sleeves, too. Black Knight can fire a dark wave of energy at Shovel Knight, but if you time an attack correctly, you can knock these back in Black Knight's direction. By making small jumps forward and slashing quickly and repeatedly with your shovel, you can knock Black Knight into a corner, at which point you can hit him repeatedly for maximum damage.

PRIDEMOOR KEEP

Description

This golden sentinel stands proudly on the western edge of the valley. King Knight, the keep's pompous impostor, staged a coup and ousted the rightful king. In the king's absence, the keep has been infested with impractical propeller rats and armed with the Enchantress's magical minions, the Wizzem and Goldarmor.

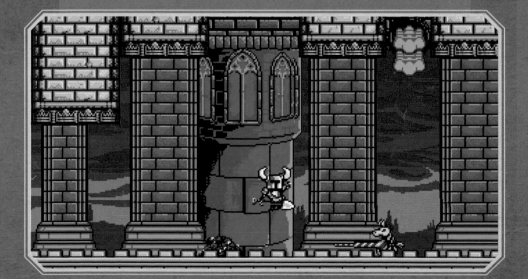

Enemies

BEETO

BLITZSTEED

PROPELLER RAT

WIZZEM

GOLDARMOR

CROWNDALIER

FIRE POT

If you walk under or stand on these ornate light fixtures, they will collapse! Watch out!

These cauldrons will dump flowing lava onto your head if you don't time your movement correctly.

SPELLBOOK

Shovel Drop onto the Spellbook, and magical pages will appear in the air. You can stand on these runes to access hard-to-reach ledges, but they disappear over time. Hit the book again to reset the timer.

Mini-Boss
Griffoth

These beloved pets of King Pridemoor, the rightful king, stand watch on the keep's rampart. Unfortunately, these birdbrains think you're an intruder, and will protect King Knight at all costs. When they breathe fire, the fireballs always move in the same pattern, so stand in the same place where you won't get caught in the blast. Jump and slash at the Griffoth's head repeatedly to defeat them but watch out for Griffoth's claw attack when you get close.

Music Sheet #23
The Halls of the Usurper

Travel left from the starting area of Pridemoor Keep to find a corridor with the Music Sheet at the end.

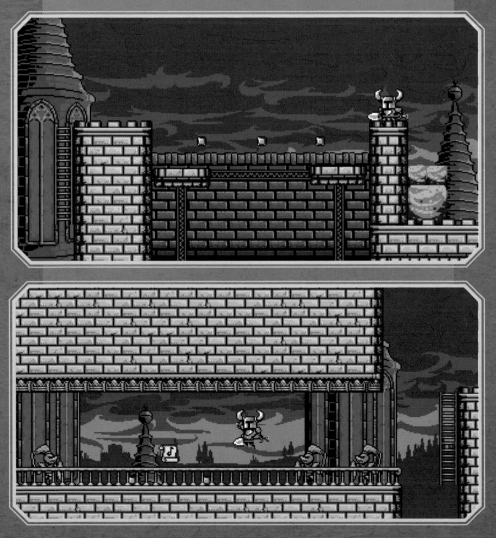

Music Sheet #24
The Decadent Dandy

When you reach the area after the first Griffoth mini-boss, travel to the next checkpoint and dig through the left wall to find a new area with the Music Sheet.

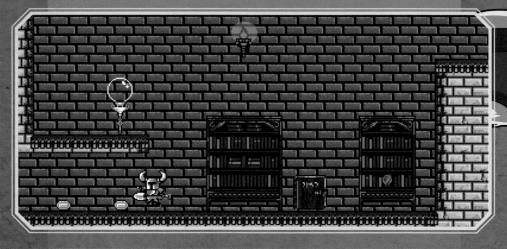

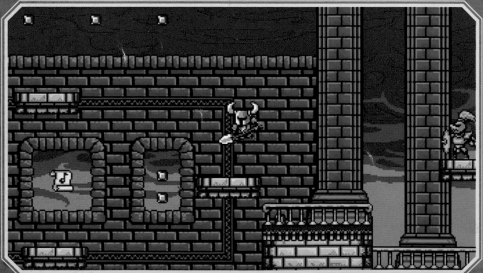

King Knight

After the Enchantress came to power, King Knight ousted the keep's rightful king and joined the Order of No Quarter. He now rules Pridemoor Keep with a gilded fist and commands a host of dangerous minions. He will do everything in his power to preserve his throne and keep Shovel Knight from knocking the false crown off his head.

This fight is fairly straightforward. King Knight makes little hops across the throne room while swinging his scepter. Slash at him with your Shovel Blade, and when he is about to pass over you, jump and Shovel Drop off him, then rush in and keep attacking. Follow him into a corner. When he smashes the ground with his cane, it stuns you and wiggling the controls will free your movement. When the horns blare and the deadly confetti falls, do your best to ignore it and keep slashing King Knight with all your might! His crown will soon clatter to the ground.

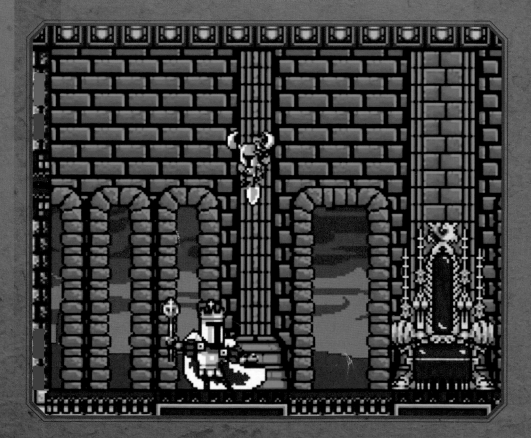

THE LICH YARD

Description

The Lich Yard was a peaceful town until the Enchantress came to power. Specter Knight overran it, and it was plunged into darkness as the townspeople fled. The only denizens left are the ghosts and skeletons that stalk the dark village.

TADVOLT

BONECLANG

BONECLANG HONCHO

LOOSE BONECLANG

HEADLESS BONECLANG

BRITTLE BONECLANG

INVISISHADE

Obstacles

BOUNCE BUSH

GRAVESTONE

Slash these green bushes and they will launch you into the air. You can Shovel Drop off of them to reach high places. You can slash them while they're in the air to go even higher!

Shovel Drop off of these for a height boost, but you may wake up an Invisishade.

Super Skeleton

These piles of bones will assemble into an ancient and imposing bone guardian. Use the terrain to avoid its jumps and when it collapses, Shovel Drop on top of it. Keep Shovel Dropping. When the Super Skeleton stands back up, you'll go up with it, but watch out for his dagger. If you stay on top, you will dispatch the Super Skeleton quickly.

Music Sheet #25
La Danse Macabre

Look for a chest directly under one of the checkpoints. See that platform made of red skeletons? It moves down if you put weight on it, so head right, find a Boneclang Honcho head, and shovel it onto the platform. This will allow you to reach the area with the chest, which contains the Music Sheet.

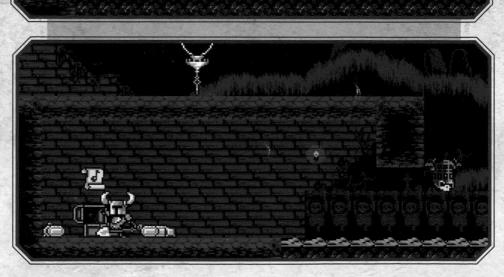

Music Sheet #26
The Apparition

In the area above the second checkpoint you'll find a pair of Bounce Bushes. Hit the one on the left twice and the one on the right once, and then you can Shovel Drop your way up onto the ledge atop the left wall. Move left into a secret area that contains the Music Sheet (and a spooky Invisishade)! Don't be afraid of the dark. Move only once you know where you can jump. Swat at the ghost to neutralize him.

Boss
Specter Knight

Specter Knight was once a thrill-seeking adventurer, eager to find fame and fortune. After falling in battle, and at the brink of his demise, Specter Knight was granted new life from an unlikely source: the Enchantress. Bound to her by the terms of their dark pact, he now serves as a loyal member of the Order of No Quarter, ruling over the Lich Yard with unwavering resolve.

Imbued with the magic granted to him by the Enchantress, Specter Knight is an enemy as deadly as he is dead. In addition to his spinning scythe, Specter Knight can use his vast necromantic powers to raise Brittle Boneclangs to fight you. He can teleport around the screen with ease. He can even plunge the stage into darkness as his health fades. Try to get behind him so you can whale on him with your Shovel Blade. If you have the Phase Locket from earlier in the level, it can help you avoid damage. Avoid his scythe attacks by jumping over him or standing on the platform once you have observed his limited patterns.

EXPLODATORIUM

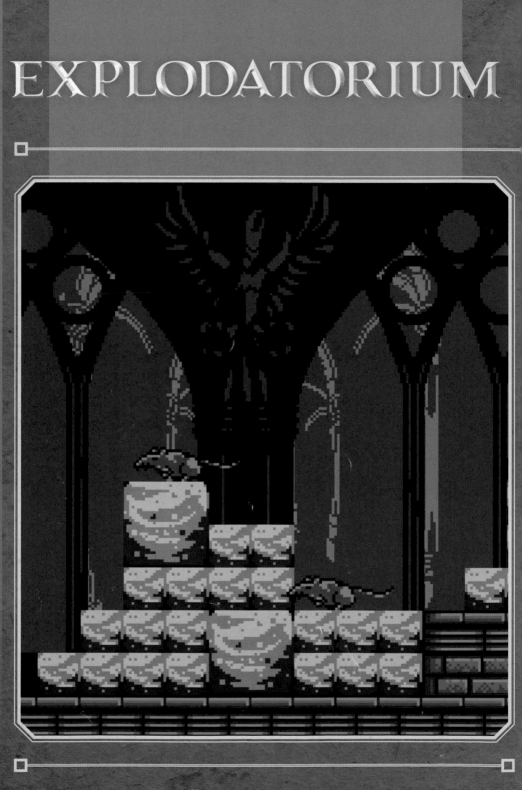

The Explodatorium is a dark alchemical lab full of bubbles and blasting. Plague Knight and his minions spend their days in dank alcoves dreaming up alchemical nightmares. Foul brews bubble in enormous beakers throughout the building, and steaming cauldrons may explode at any moment.

Enemies

BEETO

RATSPLODER

MACAWBE

PLAGUE MINION

FAIRY

BLORB

GOLDARMOR

KETTELEG

SLIMULACRA

GREEN GOLDARMOR

BURNER

PLAGUE CAULDRON

The Explodatorium is host to two different kinds of burners ready to scorch the unwary adventurer. One type is the gold, unstable burner that ignites when stepped upon and the other is the silver time-based burner that throws its flames out in a set pattern.

These cauldrons will blow their lids. If you stand on a lid, it'll shoot you into the air. Learn their patterns and use them to your advantage. Watch out for the ones with spikes.

Mini-Boss
The Alchemeister

The Alchemeister joined forces with Plague Knight to learn his potion-making ways. Now he hurls those explosive bottles at any trespassers, and if threatened, he will drink a potion of transmogrification to become an enormous white beast. Watch out for the beast's charging attacks. If you can get behind him while he is in human form, you can deal a lot of damage before he moves out of the way. Try bouncing on him successively in monster form without falling off for maximum hits.

> KILL HIM IN MONSTER FORM TO GET A TURKEY; KILL HIM IN HUMAN FORM TO GET MAGIC.

Music Sheet #29
Flowers of Antimony

Past the second checkpoint you'll find a room where fast-moving Macawbes drop potions at you. Don't let them blow up the destructible platforms at the end of this area. You need the platforms to jump onto the ceiling, which you can break through to get the Music Sheet. You can also lure Plague Minion on the right toward the Music Sheet and Shovel Drop off him to get there.

Music Sheet #30
The Vital Vitriol

In the room with the first checkpoint, knock the Ratsploders into the wall to open a secret passage in the upper right. Follow the ladder to a hidden area with a chest that has the Music Sheet.

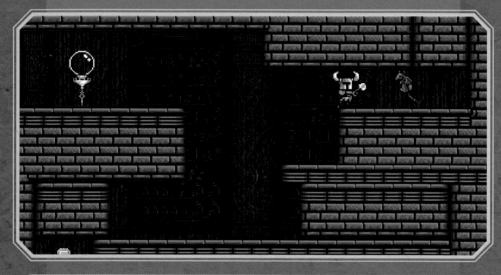

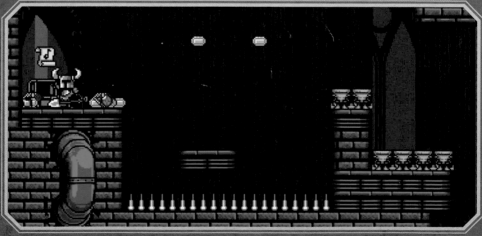

Plague Knight

Plague Knight spent a lifetime in the poorly ventilated chambers of his alchemical lab. He's willing to sacrifice everything for scientific goals. Even the other members of the Order of No Quarter keep their distance, out of fear that one of Plague Knight's volatile bottles will explode and melt their armor. Plague Knight is unpredictable, explosive, and maniacal. A worthy foe.

Plague Knight is one of the harder bosses to defeat. He jumps around like crazy, spawning cauldrons, beakers, bottles, and other obstacles. Use Chaos Orbs to catch Plague Knight as he teleports around the room. In a pinch you can bounce the bombs he throws back at him. Focus on keeping up with him and getting a few quick dig slashes in before he teleports out of your range.

IRON WHALE

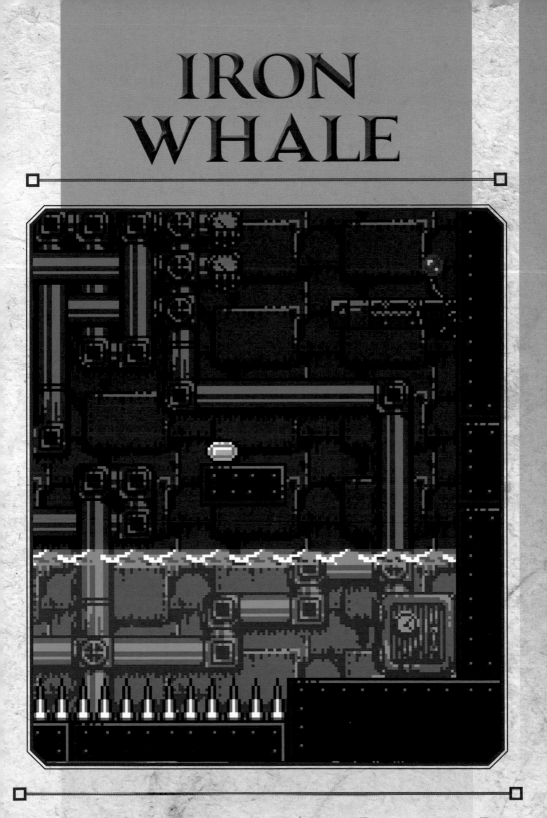

Description

The Iron Whale is a giant whale-shaped submarine that cruises through the ocean's depths, always on the hunt for treasure. The captain of this vessel is Treasure Knight, who lays claim to treasures found in sunken wrecks. It's easy to navigate the Iron Whale's rusty interior, assuming you don't mind flooded chambers and getting your armor wet.

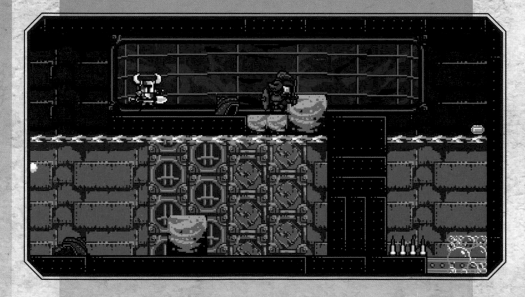

HERMITTACK

GOBCANO

PURPLE GOLDARMOR

SERPRIZE

GULPER MAGE

GRAPPS

MANTAR

Obstacles

ANCHOR

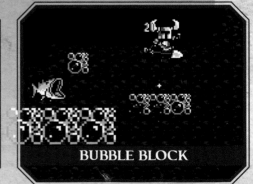

FLOATING PLATFORM

Anchors drop and then slowly rise back up. You can hop on them and go for a ride. Just make sure you're riding up and not down. Some are triggered as you get close.

When you step on these seaweed-coated platforms, they will rise quickly to the surface.

TORPEDO

BUBBLE BLOCK

Slash at the lever and go for a ride. Hop off before it explodes so it doesn't hurt you.

You can stand on these blocks, but once you do, the bubbles will start to pop. When they are gone, you will fall.

Teethalon

Below the Iron Whale on the deepest seafloor lurks Teethalon, an enormous, hungry, nasty anglerfish. Teethalon will chase unsuspecting explorers in an attempt to make them his dinner. She also draws in greedy treasure hunters with her treasure chest lure. The orb in the chest is Teethalon's only weak point. You'll have to slash it, or use one of your relics. You can also Shovel Drop off her chest to maneuver your position, but it does no damage.

Music Sheet #27
A Thousand Leagues Below

When you first see the Grapps, find a shell in the rocks on the right side of the room. Break the shell to open a secret passage. In the hidden area, make your way to the chest and then circle back. Where the first Grapps appeared, cast your fishing pole over the sparkling area to find the Music Sheet.

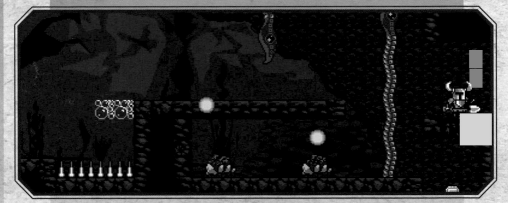

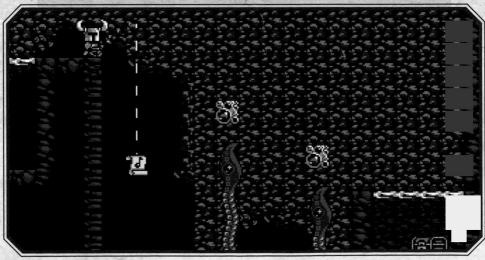

Music Sheet #28
The Bounty Hunter

Heading up the ladder after the room with the third checkpoint, you'll find a crack in the wall. Break through it and enter a secret area. Time your jumps on the Bubble Blocks correctly. Inside the chest is the Music Sheet. Use the Torpedo to return safely.

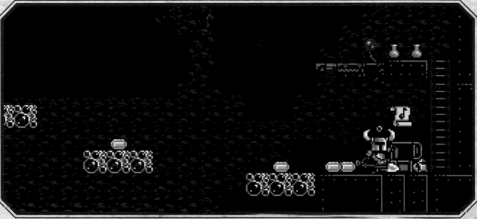

Boss
Treasure Knight

Treasure Knight, clad in his impenetrable dive suit, is captain of the Iron Whale and the greediest knight to ever explore the ocean's depths. Sunken treasure, buried treasure, floating treasure — Treasure Knight craves them all. His role in the Order of No Quarter is to maintain control of the waters throughout the valley.

Dodge the attacks from Treasure Knight's huge grapple anchor. Use the Shovel Drop wisely, as Treasure Knight has a tendency to shoot his harpoon straight up in the air. When he is low on health, Treasure Knight will create a water vortex and throw DIE-monds around. Try using the Chaos Sphere to damage him while you concentrate on avoiding his attacks. If you are caught in the chest at the center of the vortex, Treasure Knight will steal 500G from you!

LOST CITY

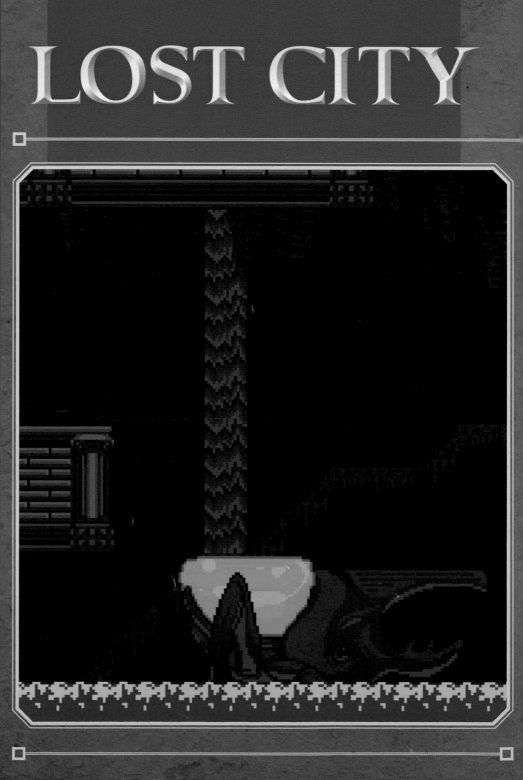

Description

The Lost City is a destination for only the hardiest of adventurers. Once a bustling metropolis, the ancient city was abandoned and subsequently sunk into a stone cavern far below the earth's surface. Ancient ruins and priceless artifacts lie within. These are guarded by Mole Knight, the great excavator who has laid claim to the vast underground domain.

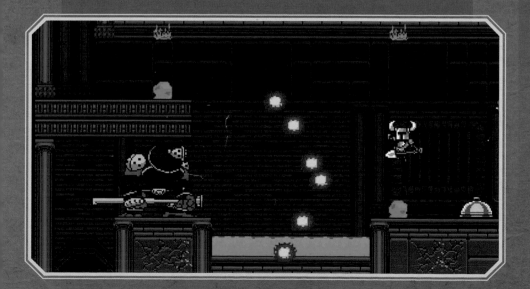

Enemies

MOLER

HOPPICLES

BIRDER

CHARFLOUNDER

BEETO

RED GOLDARMOR

BLORB

FIRE BLORB

LAVA

EXPLOSIVE BLOCK

Falling in lava will cause you to perish, but knocking green goo into the lava will temporarily make it safe to bounce on.

One slash will blow up chains of these volatile rocks. Think carefully before you attack one and don't let them blow up under your feet.

Mole Minion

These armored guardians have far-reaching golden spears. Watch their pattern to avoid the fiery blasts. Rush forward and slash at his head quickly, then jump out of the way before he charges you with a bladed thrust! Bounce on the staff when it is extended.

Lost City Creature

Big Bohto

Her abdomen is covered in bouncy goo and makes a great trampoline. Her durable exoskeleton makes her immune to lava and other hazards. But she doesn't slow down for Shovel Knight, so try and keep up!

Music Sheet #31
An Underlying Problem

In the room with the second checkpoint, don't destroy the second set of explosive blocks. Instead, use them to reach the ledge above the wall on the right side. This ledge leads to a new area where you can Shovel Drop across some Charflounders to get to the chest with the Music Sheet.

Music Sheet #32
The Claws of Fate

When you see lava that looks like a staircase, turn it into goo and jump off the top stair. Land on the ledge above the right wall, and head right to find a secret area that contains the Music Sheet.

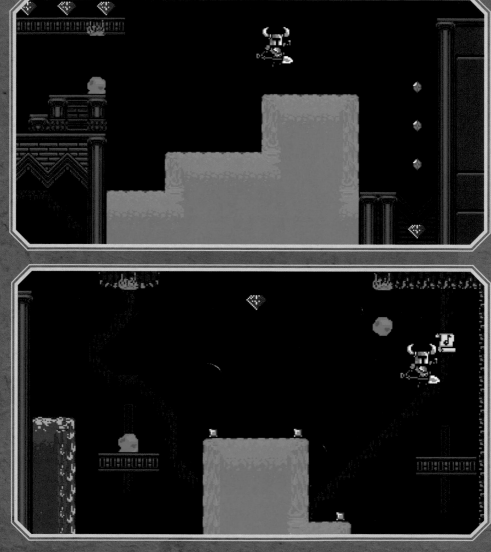

Mole Knight

The thought of a knight wielding a shovel offends Mole Knight on a deeply personal level. According to him, the claws of a mole are the only true digging instrument! Mole Knight has laid claim to the sunken metropolis known as the Lost City, and rules the underground on behalf of the Enchantress.

Mole Knight uses his claws to dig through the walls of his chamber and even to burrow through the floor. He'll burst out of the wall he jumped into, so be careful you don't get clawed. Try to Shovel Drop on him as he passes by. Slash through or jump over the walls of blocks he throws at you. When he burrows into the ground, four piles will appear on the floor. The one with Mole Knight's gold visor is the one you want to slash. He may pick up speed, but if you're fast with your shovel slashes, you will triumph. During the fire phase, he will be engulfed in flames and throw fiery rocks at you. The flashing ones can be bounced back!

CLOCKWORK TOWER

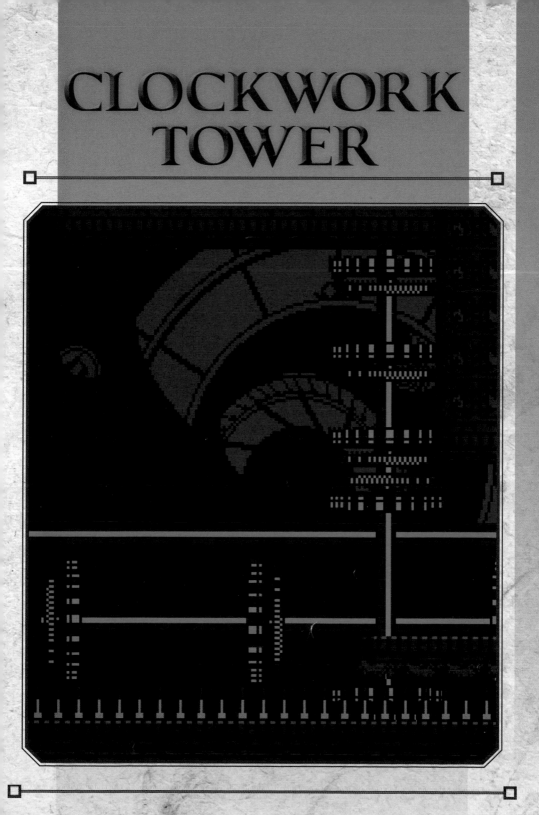

Description

The Clockwork Tower can be seen throughout the valley. If you pass by the tower's turning gears, you may even hear the clanging sounds of Tinker Knight's hammer. His dangerous traps and ominous-looking automatons all serve to guard his mechanical masterpiece, the halls of Clockwork Tower.

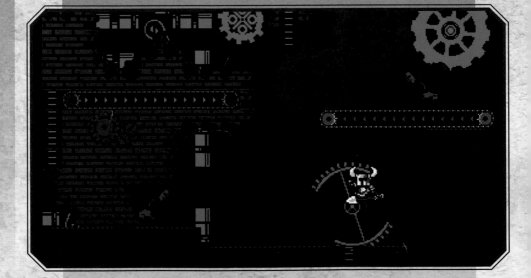

ELECTRODENT

GEAR WIZZEM

FAIRY

COGSLOTTER

GOLDARMOR

SILVER GOLDAMOR

RED GOLDARMOR

SINE DAGGER

Obstacles

ROLLING GEAR

ROLLER

DRAWBRIDGE

CONVEYOR BELT

Don't fight these rolling gears; just jump over them, or bounce on them to avoid damage.

Hopping over and over will keep you on these spiraling dangers.

These can extend over bottomless pits, so time your route carefully.

The color and direction of the arrows of each belt let you know what direction it is going. Use little hops to stay in place, and time your jumps carefully.

Music Sheet #33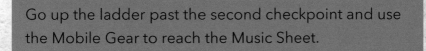
Of Devious Machinations

Go up the ladder past the second checkpoint and use the Mobile Gear to reach the Music Sheet.

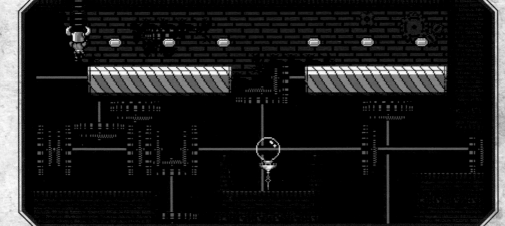

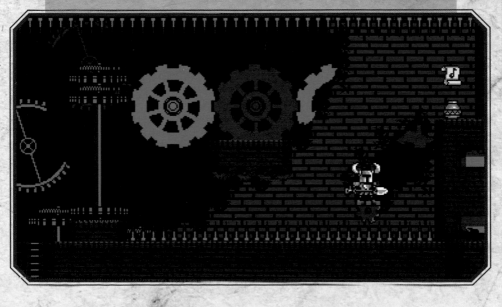

Music Sheet #34
The Schemer

In the room above the first checkpoint, go to the right, behind the Cogslotter. In the area beyond you can find the Music Sheet.

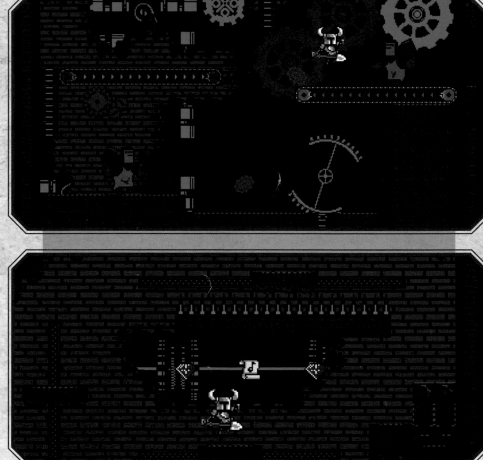

Music Sheet #35
The Destroyer

Past the third checkpoint, go under the platform where the Cogslotter is throwing gears and hop across the Rollers to reach the pink diamond. Proceed left through a dangerous secret area and go up to a room with more Cogslotters and the Music Sheet.

Boss
Tinker Knight

Tinker Knight's small stature has pushed him to create monstrous machines to fight on his behalf. He uses his trusty wrench to cobble together contraptions and to send foolish intruders running.

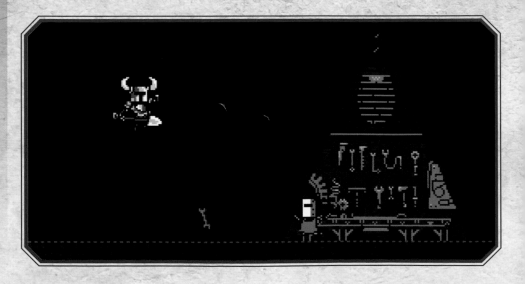

Fighting this little pipsqueak seems easy at first. He will toss wrenches at you, but you can jump to easily avoid them. Shovel Drop him when he's close, but run away if he trips and freaks out. Tinker Knight will fall quickly but don't be fooled: This is where the real fight begins. Now you'll drop into a pit where Tinker Knight has armed himself with a Tinker Tank. Jump on his missiles and up onto his roller lance. Then you can Shovel Drop on Tinker Knight's head in the robot's cockpit. It's his only weak point. Look out for the small missiles he shoots at you while you're up there. Jump back onto his shoulder after jumping on his head a few times. Make sure not to fall and avoid his rockets.

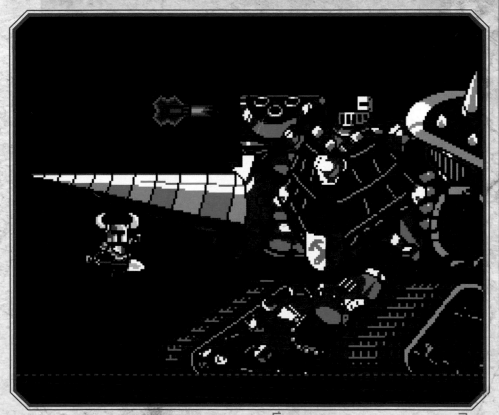

STRANDED
SHIP

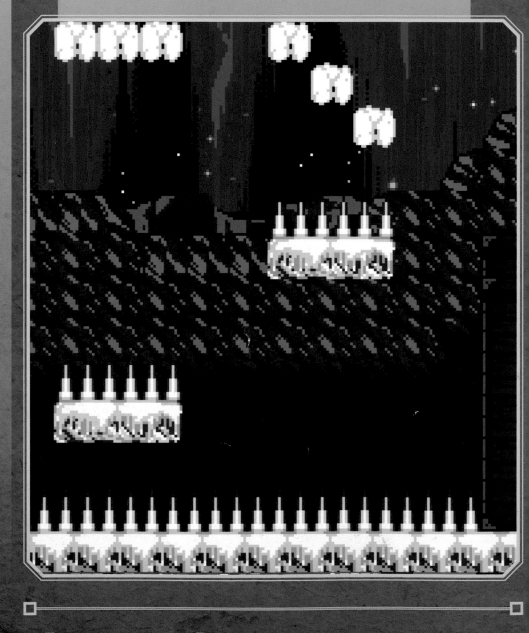

Description

Farther into the valley lies the Frozen Tundra. There lies the weathered hull of a stranded ship, trapped in the ice. The Enchantress laid claim to the Stranded Ship and convinced Polar Knight to look after it for her. He commands a crew of icy minions you will have to defeat before you face him.

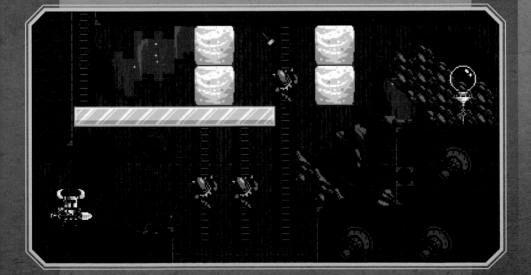

Enemies

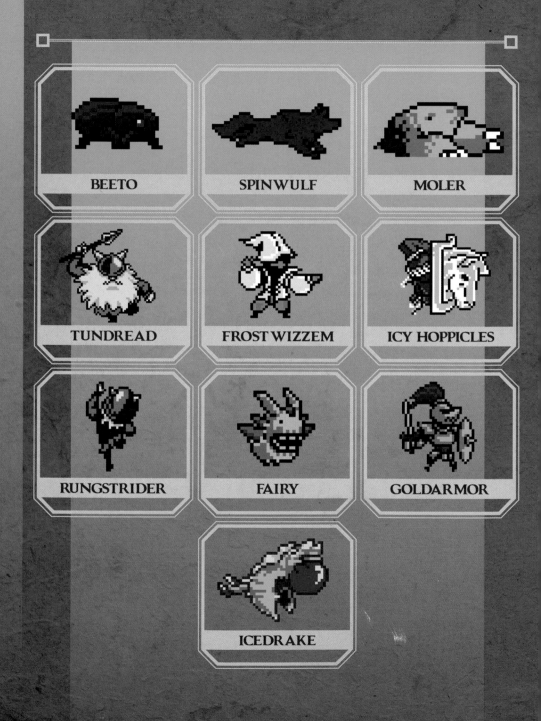

BEETO

SPINWULF

MOLER

TUNDREAD

FROST WIZZEM

ICY HOPPICLES

RUNGSTRIDER

FAIRY

GOLDARMOR

ICEDRAKE

RAINBOW BRIDGE

SNOW DRIFTS

Stand on the Rainbow Bridge and slash to move it forward. Jump while on it and it will rise. Stand still and it will sink.

These spikes have snow above them. Pass through the snow and it will fall and cover the spikes, protecting Shovel Knight's feet.

Music Sheet #36
A Cool Reception

After the fourth checkpoint, go up and head right. You'll spot the Music Sheet on an out-of-reach platform. Shovel Drop off a swooping Icedrake to reach the platform.

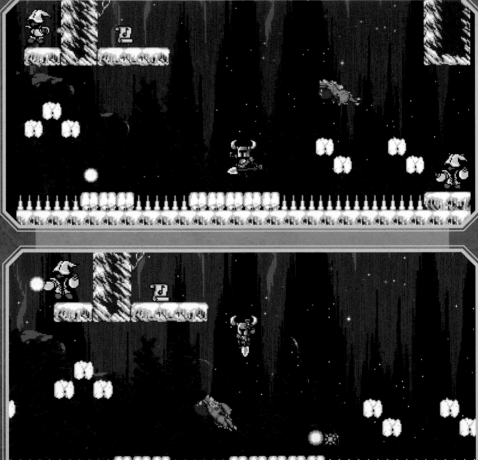

Music Sheet #37
The Stalwart

Just before Music Sheet #36, look for a Frost Wizzem on the ledge above the left wall. Defeat him and head left into a secret area. Be careful not to slip off the icy moving platforms as you make your way over the spikes to the Music Sheet.

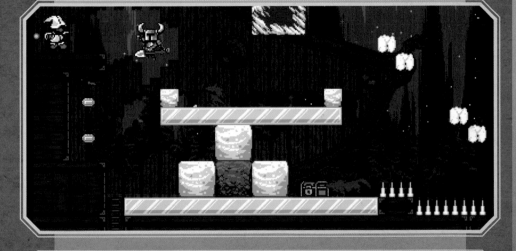

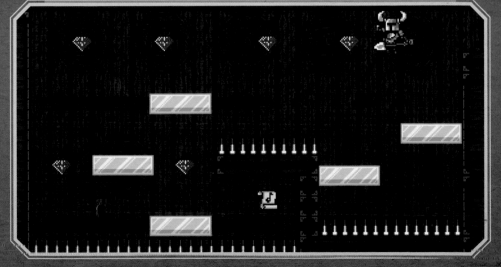

Boss
Polar Knight

Polar Knight is a man of few words, but this gruff brute has secrets he dares not reveal. He is trained in the arts of Shovelry. He fights not with a normal shovel blade, but with a custom snow shovel built to fit his massive hands. He respects strength and power. He joined the Order of No Quarter to serve the Enchantress, the most powerful being in the land.

Polar Knight has a number of devastating attacks. He will roll giant snowballs at you, leap into the air and crash down, and even break the ice under your feet, revealing deadly spikes! The Shovel Drop works well, but Polar Knight will raise his shovel to deflect you if you hit him twice. Avoid falling on the spikes at all costs: If required, absorb blows or use the Phase Locket. If you get hit, your invulnerability time can provide some room to get a few attacks in. Keep fighting and eventually the giant will fall.

FLYING MACHINE

The Flying Machine patrols the skies above the valley, menacing townships and providing reinforcements to the Order of No Quarter. The large propellers on top of the airship's masts keep it aloft, but be careful as you traverse the Flying Machine. One aggressive gust of wind, and you'll be taking a nosedive thousands of feet to your doom!

Enemies

FLOATSOME

BEETO

LIGHTNING WIZZEM

HOVER MEANIE

HOVERHAFT

PROPELLER RAT

FAN

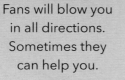

CANNONBALL

Fans will blow you in all directions. Sometimes they can help you.

These cannonballs look dangerous but you can Shovel Drop right on top of them. Use them to cross big gaps.

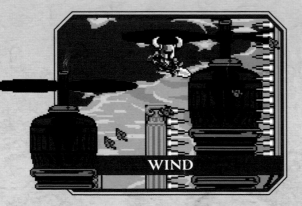

WIND

Even the wind has it out for you! Be careful not to get blown off course. The wind direction changes are timed. Watch for patterns.

Mini-Boss
The Dinghy Dropper

Propeller Knight's most elite Hoverhaft soldiers are promoted to pedal and pilot the Dinghy Dropper. Be careful as it flies and then drops quickly to the ground. Jump when the Dinghy Dropper hits the ground, or Shovel Knight will be stunned. If you are stunned, be sure to press all the buttons rapidly to escape damage. When the Dinghy Dropper throws bombs at you, knock them back toward the airship to damage it! Avoid Shovel Dropping on the propellers as they can damage you.

Music Sheet #38
High Above the Land

Climb the long section of ladders in this level, then fight the Lightning Wizzem on the right side. Break through the wall behind him to go up a hidden ladder. Use the Propeller Dagger to cross a large gap and reach the Music Sheet.

Music Sheet #39
The Spin Controller

When a Hover Meanie appears from below you, over a large gap, you'll notice two fans pointing upward on the right side. Fall from the previous screen and use your momentum to get there. It's in this area where Chester will sell you the Propeller Dagger. Fly to the right over the obstacles and down one screen. You'll see sparkles over a pit here. Go fishing and find the Music Sheet.

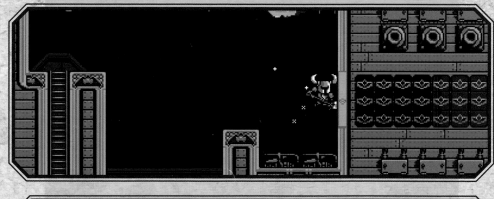

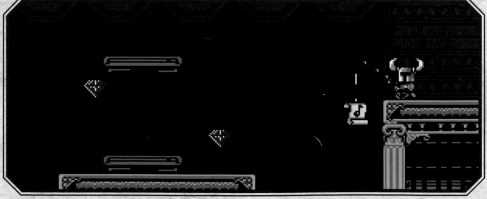

Boss
Propeller Knight

This debonair daredevil captains the Flying Machine, an airship that rules the skies over the Valley. He duels with a rapier as sharp as his tongue and whizzes through the air with his Heli-Helmet. He's kind of a jerk, but isn't he charming?

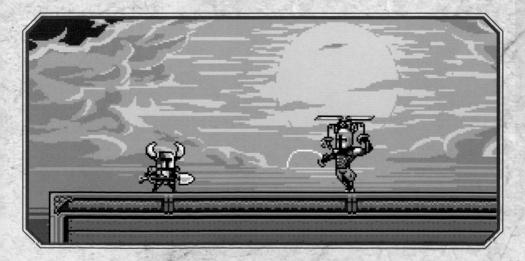

When on the ground, fight Propeller Knight blade to blade. Hit him as he lunges at you. When he takes to the skies, use the Throwing Anchor to reach him. Be sure to make your throws count! You only have so much magic. When his health is low, watch for falling cannonballs that will create pits in the floor. Avoid Shovel Dropping on his head. He has a special attack that blows you up into the air and he will attempt to skewer you as you return from the sky.

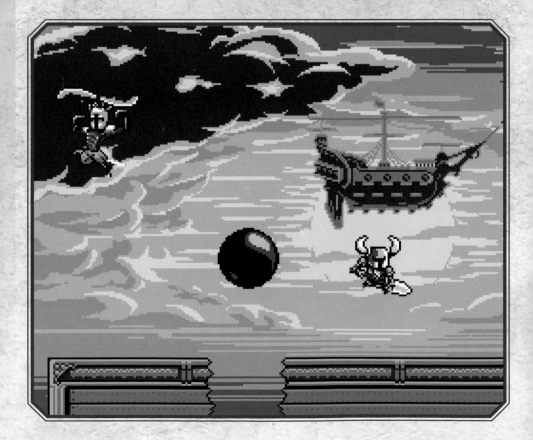

TOWER OF FATE I:
ENTRANCE

Description

You've finally made it! There's not much farther to go! The Tower of Fate is a dark beacon of the Enchantress's power. It is filled with evil magic. Getting inside the tower is your first objective, and even that will prove to be a great challenge. The rampart is treacherous and crawling with enemies, but if you make it through the front door, you'll be close to your final goal.

CHARFLOUNDER

WIZZEM

MOLER

PROPELLER RAT

BONECLANG

DARK GRIFFOTH

PLAGUE MINION

FAIRY

GOLDARMOR

HOVER MEANIE

LIQUID SAMURAI

DIVEDRAKE

Music Sheet #40
The Fateful Return

In the middle of the dark and rainy area, look for a sparkling pit next to the Purple Goldarmor. Use the Fishing Rod in the sparkling pit to pull up the Music Sheet.

Black Knight

Black Knight returns to guard the entrance to the Tower of Fate. He refuses to join the Enchantress, but he won't let Shovel Knight hurt her either. The Enchantress gives Black Knight a taste of the power she wields, making Shovel Knight's adversary devilishly dangerous.

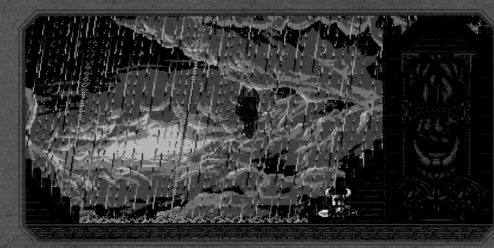

In your final battle with Black Knight, he will begin with an assault of dark waves. Avoid him at this moment as you can't hit him during the assault. After a few hits he will sprout monstrous wings and take to the skies, flinging fiery feathers at you. Then he will conjure great meteors to strike the rampart. Stay clear of these. You can bounce on the meteors in the ground to attack him with Shovel Drops. When he sprouts his wings, hop on top of him and Shovel Drop to get in some extra hits.

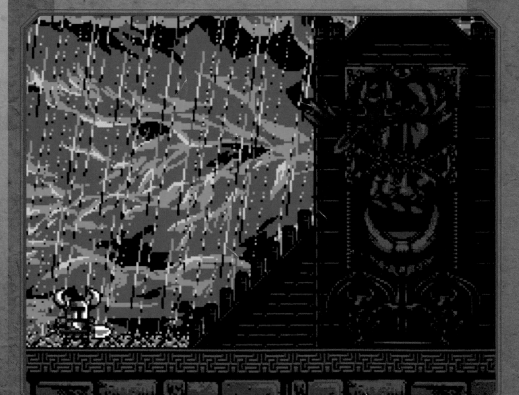

TOWER OF FATE II:
ASCENT

Description

The Enchantress filled the Tower of Fate with traps and creatures of all types. Lava pools and bottomless pits abound. If you are courageous enough to make it to the top, what will be waiting for you?!

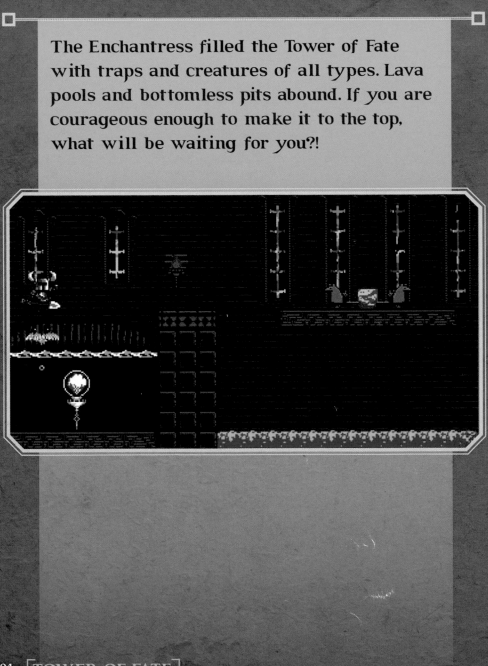

SERPRIZE

FLOATSOME

ELECTRODENT

LIQUID SAMURAI

SILVER GOLDARMOR

BLORB

WIZZEM

HOVER MEANIE

RATSPLODER

Music Sheet #41
The Inner Struggle

After the third checkpoint, navigate the rising room (don't get squished!) and you'll see the Music Sheet on the right end of a long passage. Move quickly, grab it, and get out fast!

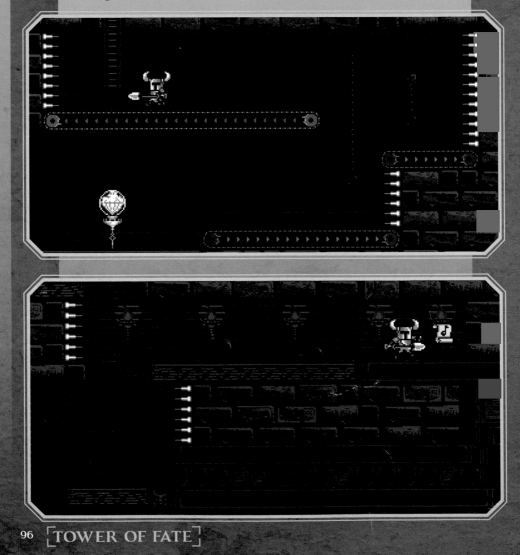

Music Sheet #42
The Forlorn Sanctum

Before continuing to the third checkpoint, use the bird statue to break through the wall in the upper right. There, you'll find the Music Sheet.

Battle Royale

After being defeated by Shovel Knight, the eight members of the Order of No Quarter retreated to the Tower of Fate to regroup and have a meal of mourning. When Shovel Knight interrupts their mealtime, they leap into action for the ultimate battle royale!

The Order of No Quarter will attack you one at a time, but you won't be able to predict the order in which they will attempt to quarter you. Make sure your Troupple Chalices are filled. Don't forget to take advantage of the new relics and skills you acquired since the last time you battled each boss. Only eat the turkey right before you need it. A new platter arrives with each new boss and magic drops in with every other platter.

TOWER
OF FATE

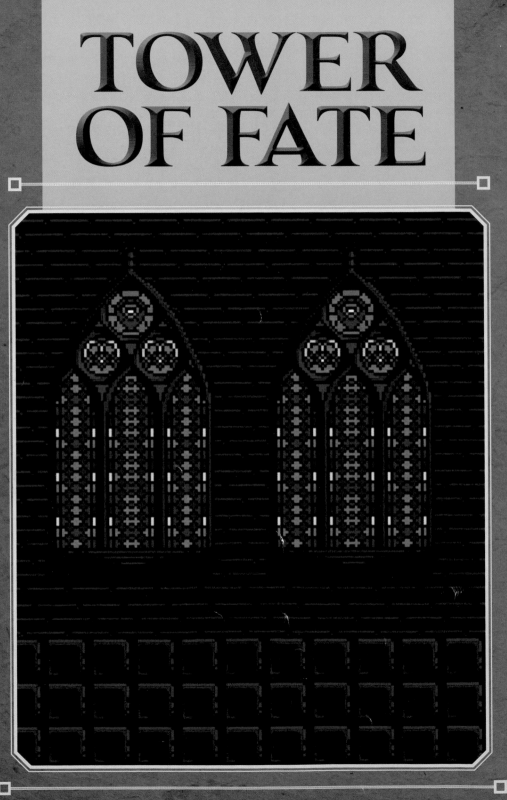

Here you will face your greatest battle!
Indeed, the very walls of the Tower will
reach out and attack you. Pay attention and
focus. Everything you've done has prepared
you for this moment.

Mini-Boss
Attacking Blocks

Try standing on the far right platform. Dodge the blocks that fly past you and Shovel Drop onto the ones that would hit you. Try using the Phase Locket to avoid them.

Mini-Boss
Rising Blocks

Move carefully across the blocks as they rise up to support you. Be courageous.

I CAN'T BELIEVE SHE STOLE MY MUSIC.

After you escape the attacking blocks and drop into the dark room, go left over the lava and you'll find the final five Music Sheets among some other goodies.

The Enchantress

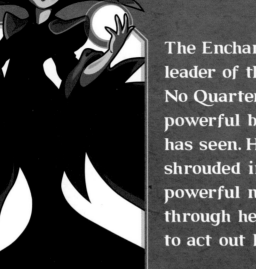

The Enchantress is the leader of the Order of No Quarter and the most powerful being this valley has seen. Her origin is shrouded in mystery, but powerful magic flows through her, allowing her to act out her evil whims.

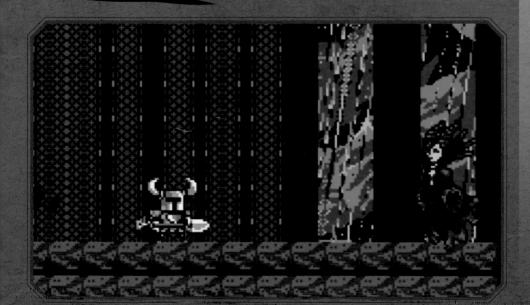

The Enchantress's dark magic attacks can destroy the blocks you are standing on. You can knock these attacks back at her with your Shovel Blade. Your relics will come in handy here. To cross large gaps, use the Propeller Dagger. When the Enchantress flies underneath the platform, hit her from above with your Throwing Anchor if you're feeling lucky. Prioritize staying in areas with lots of blocks. When you see an opening and are on safe ground, leap in close and strike. Take care not to break the blocks under you by Shovel Dropping onto them. When she raises new blocks to attack you, move closer to the gaps so she will fill them in. Use a combination of Shovel Drops and slashes to maximize damage.

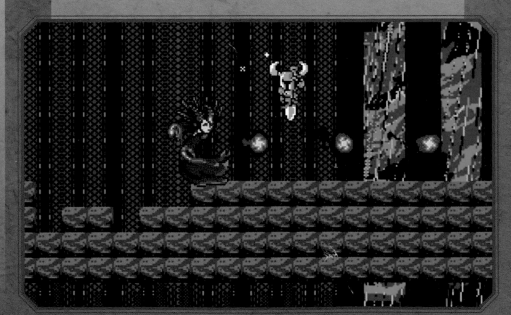

The Remnant of Fate

It is discovered that the Enchantress was Shield Knight and now Shield Knight joins the fray to help you combat the full force of the Enchantress's evil power. Stay close to Shield Knight throughout the battle. She will protect you from the boss's barrages of energy balls.

When Shield Knight leaps into the air and holds her shield above her head, leap into the air and Shovel Drop off the shield to reach the boss's head (its only weak point). If you get split up, you can use the Phase Locket to avoid the energy balls. Watch your landings! The Remnant of Fate will smash holes in the floor. Shovel Dropping makes her move away but slashing beats her the fastest. Bounce on the shield, slash and repeat. After 3 consecutive Shovel Drops, she will attempt to avoid a fourth. If you need help avoiding pits or need an extra boost, use your Propeller Dagger. Try using a combination of slashes and Shovel Drops to maximize your damage.

RELICS

FLARE WAND

MAGIC: 4

STAGE: Pridemoor Keep

STAGE PRICE: 1,000

VILLAGE PRICE: 2,000

HOW TO FIND: After the second checkpoint, go down to the room with the cutout of Shovel Knight on the far wall. Make your way across the gap, match your pose to the cutout, and stand still. You'll enter a secret room. Cross the high crowndaliers and get the Flare Wand from the Blue Chest, and then use the lower crowndaliers to return.

EFFECT: This magic wand shoots balls of fire. Great for far away enemies.

TIP: IF YOU CHOOSE NOT TO BUY THE RELICS IN THE STAGE, CHESTER SELLS THEM IN THE VILLAGE FOR A HIGHER PRICE.

PHASE LOCKET

MAGIC: 8

STAGE: The Lich Yard

STAGE PRICE: 1,000

VILLAGE PRICE: 2,000

HOW TO FIND: Between the second and third checkpoints, you will drop into a room with two Boneclangs. Shovel Drop off the left Boneclang onto the ledge and head left. Walk the upper path to the Blue Chest, where Chester will sell you the Phase Locket. Use the relic to return on the bottom path.

EFFECT: The Phase Locket allows you to fade into a dimension of immaterial existence for a short time, allowing you to hover in midair, walk on spikes, and pass through enemies. Good for bosses, hazards, and repeated use.

DUST KNUCKLES

MAGIC: 2

STAGE: Lost City

STAGE PRICE: 3,000

VILLAGE PRICE: 3,500

HOW TO FIND: When you reach the third checkpoint, break through the wall to the left and you'll find the Blue Chest containing the Dust Knuckles. On your way back out of the room, break through the stones with the relic to collect a ton of jewels.

EFFECT: The Dust Knuckles allow you to bust through dirt blocks in rapid succession, even if those stones are hanging from the ceiling! Good for repeated attacks on bosses.

THROWING ANCHOR

MAGIC: 6

STAGE: Iron Whale

STAGE PRICE: 3,000

VILLAGE PRICE: 3,500

HOW TO FIND: Defeat Teethalon, and the Blue Chest she drops will contain the Throwing Anchor.

EFFECT: You can fling the Throwing Anchor up in a curving arc. If you're clever, you can use the up and down nature of the arc to hit multiple enemies in one throw or even the same enemy twice. Great for bosses that float and fly above and below you.

ALCHEMY COIN

MAGIC: 8

STAGE: Explodatorium

STAGE PRICE: 3,000

VILLAGE PRICE: 3,500

HOW TO FIND: After the first checkpoint, you'll reach the end of a long room with many Plague Cauldrons. Hop off the last Plague Cauldron, Shovel Drop off one of the Fairies flying there, and land on the ledge to the right. Break through the wall past the dirt blocks, and in the secret room beyond you will find the Blue Chest containing the Alchemy Coin.

EFFECT: The Alchemy Coin spins along the floor and turns enemies to gold. Science! Great for weak enemies, but not bosses.

MOBILE GEAR

MAGIC: 6

STAGE: Clockwork Tower

STAGE PRICE: 3,000

VILLAGE PRICE: 3,500

HOW TO FIND: Climb up a few floors past the first checkpoint until you reach the hall with the Red Goldarmor guarding the way. Break through the top left wall to enter a secret area. Make your way left over the platforms, and then use the Mobile Gear along the spikes below to get back.

EFFECT: Place the Mobile Gear on the ground. You can hop on the Mobile Gear to get a ride. Jump on it to take off in a straight line, bowling over enemies. You can hop on the Mobile Gear and go for a ride. Great for riding safely over spikes.

WAR HORN

MAGIC: 20

STAGE: Stranded Ship

STAGE PRICE: 4,000

VILLAGE PRICE: 5,000

HOW TO FIND: In the room above the third checkpoint, break through the wall on the left side and knock the snow onto the spiked platforms to make them safe to cross. The Blue Chest on the left side contains the War Horn (and a very chilly Chester).

EFFECT: Though each use of the War Horn costs a lot of magic, it is a very potent weapon that will heavily damage enemies surrounding you. It does not do much damage to bosses and mini-bosses. Try using it during a campfire dream sequence.

PROPELLER DAGGER

MAGIC: 4

STAGE: Flying Machine

STAGE PRICE: 4,000

VILLAGE PRICE: 5,000

HOW TO FIND: In the room above the second checkpoint, there are two fans keeping you from the secret area. Use the Mobile Gear to ride over the fans, or climb up the ladder to the next room then drop down, holding right, and duck into the secret area. Your downward momentum will allow you to fight the fans' power.

EFFECT: Once you have the Propeller Dagger, you'll be able to zip through the air, stab enemies in mid-flight, and cross large gaps. Great for moving across gaps in tandem with Shovel Drops.

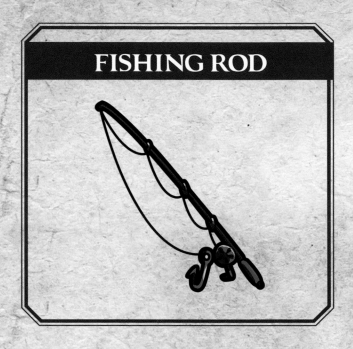

FISHING ROD

MAGIC: 6

STAGE: First Village Basement

STAGE PRICE: N/A

VILLAGE PRICE: 1,250

HOW TO FIND: You can buy the Fishing Rod from Chester in the Village.

EFFECT: Whenever you see sparkles sparkling over a pit, you can fish in that pit and pull up items. Maybe it will be food, or maybe it will be treasure! Great for recovering lost treasure after Shovel Knight has fallen in battle. You can fish in places without sparkles, too. Try this when you are low on health.

CHAOS SPHERE

MAGIC: 6

STAGE: First Village Basement

STAGE PRICE: N/A

VILLAGE PRICE: 2,500

HOW TO FIND: You can buy the Chaos Sphere from Chester in the Village.

EFFECT: The Chaos Sphere is a green orb that bounces across the screen damaging any enemy that gets in its way. Great for almost all bosses as a Chaos Sphere can perform multiple hits while you also attack with your Shovel Blade.

RELIC COURSES

Forest of Phasing

The Forest of Phasing is filled with treasure, but it cannot be completed until you have the Phase Locket. Using this special relic, you can make it past the spikes and other obstacles.

The Forest of Phasing is unlocked once you defeat Specter Knight.

#18: THE ADVENTURE AWAITS CAN BE FOUND IN THE TREASURE CHEST AT THE END OF THE RELIC COURSE.

Enemies

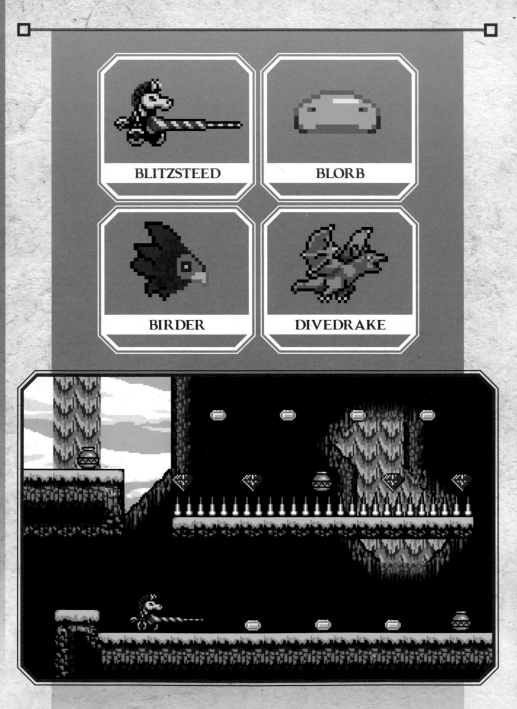

BLITZSTEED

BLORB

BIRDER

DIVEDRAKE

Knuckler's Quarry

The Knuckler's Quarry is filled with treasure, but it cannot be completed until you have the Dust Knuckles. Using this special relic, you can make it past the large gaps and Dirt Block obstacles.

The Knuckler's Quarry is unlocked once you open the second section of the valley.

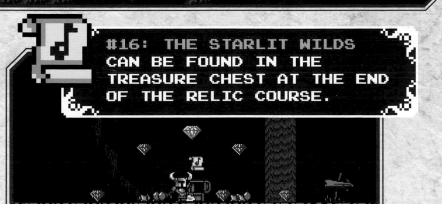

#16: THE STARLIT WILDS CAN BE FOUND IN THE TREASURE CHEST AT THE END OF THE RELIC COURSE.

Enemies

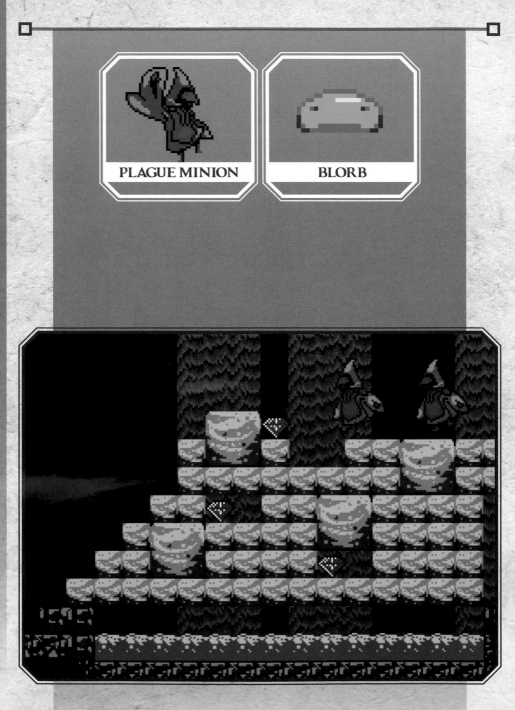

PLAGUE MINION

BLORB

Frigid Flight

The treasure in Frigid Flight is tough to get. It cannot be completed until you have the Propeller Dagger. Using this special relic, you can make it over the large pits and collect treasure floating in midair.

Frigid Flight is unlocked once you open the third section of the valley.

#17: REQUIEM OF SHIELD KNIGHT CAN BE FOUND HOVERING ABOVE THE TREASURE CHEST AT THE END OF THE RELIC COURSE.

Enemies

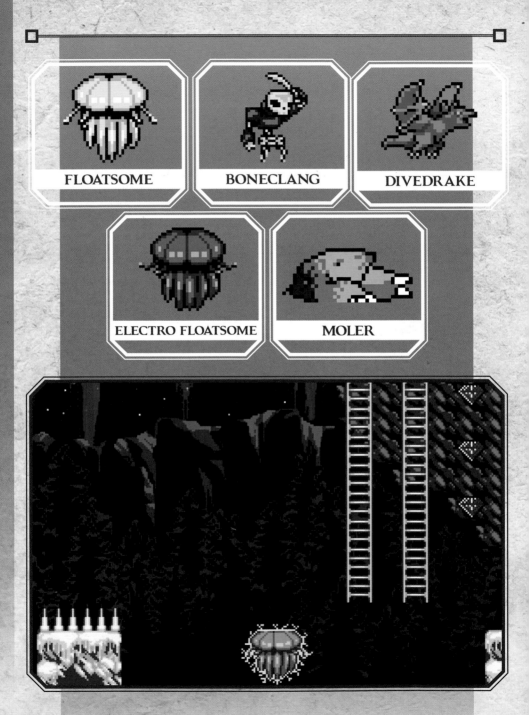

FLOATSOME

BONECLANG

DIVEDRAKE

ELECTRO FLOATSOME

MOLER

Plains Encounter

Plains Encounter is a special stage that looks like the Plains. It is marked by a Goldarmor on the map. This stage is filled with extra treasure, so pick up as much as you can. Don't be afraid of Shovel Dropping off the Divedrake to get hard to reach treasure.

Enemies

BLORB

DIVEDRAKE

BONECLANG

Pridemoor Keep Treasury

Pridemoor Keep Treasury is a loot stage that unlocks after you defeat King Knight. It is marked by a pink gem on the map. This stage moves at a set pace. If you can't proceed with the screen, you'll be knocked into a pit. Pick up as much extra treasure as you can here.

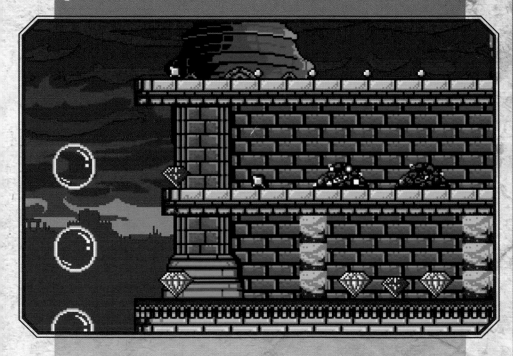

Enemies

Advance with the scrolling screen. This is dangerous because you can get caught by the scrolling screen and knocked into a pit.

Iron Whale Hidden Cache

Iron Whale Hidden Cache is a loot stage that unlocks after you defeat Treasure Knight. Like Pridemoor Keep Treasury, it is marked by a pink gem on the map. You will need to perfect your Shovel Drops to cross the row of Grapps!

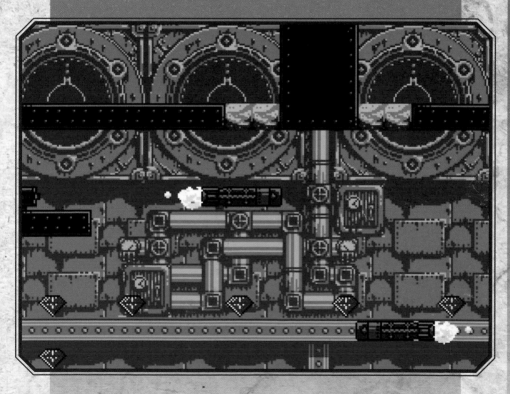

Enemies

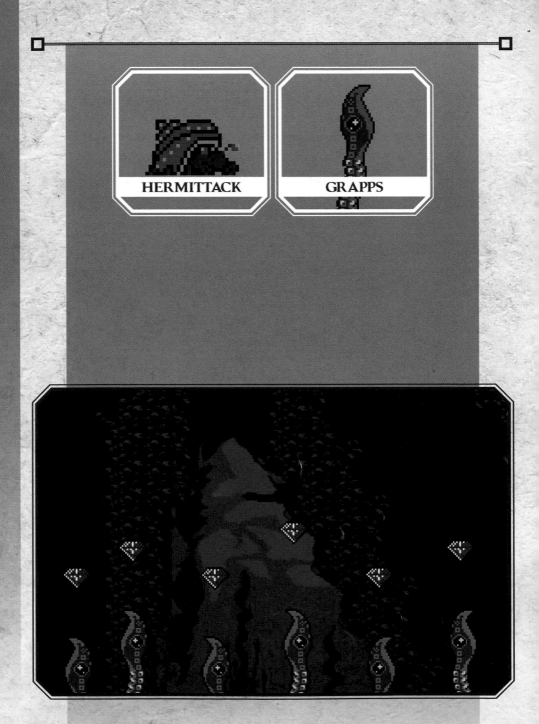

HERMITTACK

GRAPPS

Lich Yard
Encounter

Lich Yard Encounter is a loot stage that unlocks after you complete the second section of the valley. It is marked by a Goldarmor on the map. Be careful not to Shovel Drop into the pit when clearing dirt blocks.

Enemies

FIRE BLORB

GOLDARMOR

MOLER

BONECLANG

SUPER SKELETON

TROUPPLE POND

This tranquil pond is home to the great Troupple King! No enemies here, just dancing fish-apples, their benevolent ruler, and jazzy music. The Troupple King will fill your Troupple Chalices with the ichor of your choice. You must buy Troupple Chalices from the Troupple Acolyte.

Troupple King

You've never heard of the Troupple King?! Half trout and half apple! Pronounced like "mouthful"!

ICHOR OF RENEWAL

This red ichor will fully restore your health and magic.

ICHOR OF BOLDNESS

This blue ichor makes you invincible for ten seconds.

ICHOR OF FORTUNE

This gold ichor will draw all treasure to you for sixty seconds. You'll have tons of gold in no time!

HALL OF CHAMPIONS

The Hall of Champions was built as a monument to those who founded this great land. To get inside, you'll need to pay the Ticketer a fee of 5,000 gold. Although it's expensive, you'll make more inside. Invisishades lurk everywhere, and the only way to defeat them is to hit them with the Light Orbs found lying around the hall. Defeat them all to make the Big Creep appear.

#14: THE DONOR'S DESPAIR CAN BE FOUND IN A HIDDEN ROOM TO THE LEFT.

#15: BACKED INTO A CORNER CAN BE FOUND IN A HIDDEN ROOM TO THE RIGHT.

The Big Creep

The Big Creep is said to haunt the Hall of Champions.
Once you find him by defeating all the Invisishades,
you can defeat him as you did the smaller Invisishades,
with Light Orbs. When you have done enough damage
to the Big Creep, he will summon Floating Skulls. Stay
out of their way as they will spit out skull projectiles. Hit
the Light Orbs twice in the air to knock them higher to
defeat him.

SHORTCUT?

Deeper into the valley is a peaceful area where you can find a catapult. This will let you get back to the Village in a jiffy if you want to stock up on gear.

SAFE AREAS

VILLAGE

THIS QUIET PROVINCIAL TOWN IS HOME TO MANY HELPFUL ALLIES AND CURIOUS VILLAGERS.

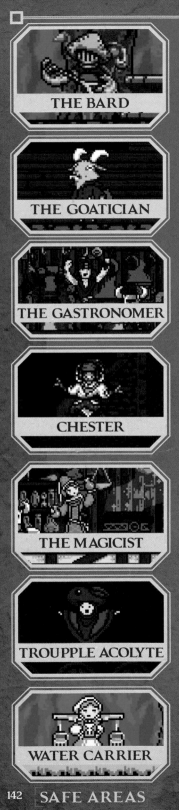

THE BARD

Hey, that's me! I've lost all my Song Scrolls. I will pay you handsomely if you can get them back to me.

THE GOATICIAN

The Goatician can't decide what to extend: his health or his magic. Why not buy his meal ticket and help narrow his options?

THE GASTRONOMER

This guy can cook up some tasty meals. If you've got Meal Tickets, he will feed you and increase your maximum health permanently! His food tastes that good.

CHESTER

Chester is always getting himself caught in Blue Chests while finding relics. Free him and he'll give you a discount on his treasures. He'll also sell his wares in the Village but at a higher price.

THE MAGICIST

Chug this lady's magical potions to permanently increase your maximum magic. Though she has a funny way of talking, she can be a big help.

TROUPPLE ACOLYTE

This fanatic hangs out in the tavern dressed like a fish (or is it a piece of fruit?). He seems to worship the Troupple King and will sell you Troupple Chalices for 1,500 gold.

WATER CARRIER

This hard-working lass can help Shovel Knight reach new hights by jumping off her shoulder.

CROAKER

Croaker is a friendly punster who is always eager to cheer up Shovel Knight with some punny croaks.

DEPOSED KING

Poor King! He once ruled Pridemoor Keep, but now he rules nothing but a lone barstool.

THE DANCING GIRL

This young lady has taken Specter Knight's rise to power pretty hard. After you defeat him, she will dance and give you Music Sheet #11.

GRANDMA SWAMP

This gifted fortune teller knows all—just don't call her a witch! She will tell you how many Dig Piles you've dug, how much gold you've acquired, the times you've died, and the total time spent playing.

MONA

There may be more to her than meets the eye. Find her after breaking through a wall to the left of the Juice Bar. Improve at her game by focusing on the sparkling potion jars!

HEDGE FARMER

This skeptical hedgehog won't believe you're the real deal until you show off your digging skills.

THE VILLAGE IS ALSO HOME
TO ALL SORTS OF COLORFUL
CHARACTERS. HERE ARE
A FEW OF THE ONES YOU
MIGHT MEET.

HOOP KID

VILLAGER

ADVENTURER

GRIZZLED SEER

KNIGHT

LADY KNIGHT

ADVENTURER

MAIDEN

DEER LADY

GATHERER

BAG FELLOW

PLAYING KID

ARMOR OUTPOST

THE ARMOR OUTPOST IS WHERE AIRSHIPS MOOR. A FEW BOUTIQUES AND OTHER SHOPS HAVE CROPPED UP AROUND THE MOORING. THERE ARE MANY FRIENDLY PEOPLE IN THE ARMOR OUTPOST (AND SOME NOT SO FRIENDLY). HERE ARE A FEW OF THE PEOPLE AND PLACES YOU'LL FIND.

PLAZA

This is a gathering place for the residents of the Armor Outpost.
Be sure to find all the Music Sheets here.

WALLACE

Wallace guards the Armor Outpost.

TOADER

This grumpy amphibian needs some cheering up. Maybe you could tell him a joke . . . or ten?

MARY SWEETS

This blonde beauty has a heart for romance, but she has trouble deciding. She has crushes on everyone in the Order of No Quarter, but her brightest candle burns for Shovel Knight.

#8: COURAGE UNDER FIRE CAN BE FOUND AT THE TOP OF A HOUSE.

#9: BUCKLERS AND BONNETS CAN BE FOUND ON TOP OF THE AIRSHIP ONCE YOU HAVE VISITED THE CATAPULT.

AERIAL ANVIL

The Aerial Anvil is a floating barge that has anchored at the Armor Outpost. I'm sure you can find some good deals inside!

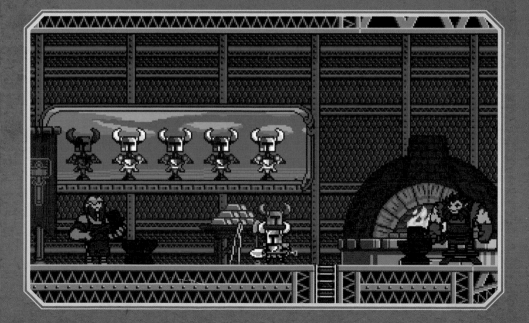

The Armorer

This burly blacksmith will fit you with all sorts of special sets of armor. Don't worry. Once you purchase a set of armor, you can swap to an old set at any time.

STALWART PLATE

Cost: 0

Description: Shovel Knight begins the game with this armor. It's comfortable!

FINAL GUARD

Cost: 3,000

Description: This red armor allows you to lose less treasure when you fall in battle.

CONJURER'S COAT

Cost: 4,000

Description: This purple mail is for heroes confident in magic usage. It increases your maximum magic, but you will more damage to your health. This armor is a double-edged sword.

DYNAMO MAIL

Cost: 6,000

Description: Performing two consecutive Shovel Drops in this armor builds up a charge inside your Shovel Blade, which you can then unleash in a doubly powerful attack!

MAIL OF MOMENTUM

Cost: 6,000

Description: This heavy black plate mail reduces how much enemies can knock you back, which is important for, you know, not falling into pits and plummeting to your death. But the extra weight means it can be hard to slow down.

ORNATE PLATE

Cost: 8,000

Description: This stylish gold armor offers no practical benefits, but you sure look good wearing it!

Shovel Smith

An expert crafter of shovel-based weaponry, Shovel Smith can enhance your Shovel Blade with royal upgrades.

Upgrade: Trench Blade

Cost: 3,000

Description: This heavy-duty blade allows you to dig up dig piles quickly with one scoop.

Upgrade: Charge Handle

Cost: 4,000

Description: By holding down the attack button, you can charge your Shovel Blade with power. Release the button to release a powerful attack, increasing your range and doubling your damage.

Upgrade: Drop Spark

Cost: 6,000

Description: When at full health, you can scrape your Shovel Blade along the ground to create a wave of sparks that will crash into enemies from a distance.

YOPPLER

This musical dwarf loves to blow his horn, but he longs for a partner to play a duet with. Once you get the War Horn relic, you should try to help him out.

AIRSHIP ENTHUSIAST

This fine fellow is a rich man who used to own an airship.

AERIAL ANVIL ROOF

After Mole Knight, Plague Knight and Treasure Knight have been defeated, a catapult will appear here, allowing you to travel quickly between the Village and the Armor Outpost.

HORSE SCHOLAR

This sophisticated stallion operates the catapult and has a love for ballistic physics.

THE FANCY SHOP

As its name implies, the Fancy Shop houses the fanciest goods in the valley. It is operated by Mr. Hat.

MR. HAT

The hat-wearing, sword-wielding proprietor of the Fancy Shop has a few surprises in store. Read more about him on page 156.

LEO

Leo appreciates the fine things in life and is a compulsive shopper. It's no surprise he finds himself a little short on cash. Give him gold!

PEACOCK GENT

This peacock may be a scam artist, but you should pay him 1,000 gold anyway and see what happens.

DOLLY

Dolly works hard so she can doll herself up and feel pretty, but she cannot afford the beret she wants most of all.

ARMOR OUTPOST IS A BUSTLING TOWNSHIP. WANDER AROUND AND YOU'LL MEET EVEN MORE INTERESTING FOLKS!

Wandering Travelers

THE VALLEY IS FILLED
WITH WANDERERS,
EXPLORERS, VAGABONDS,
AND HIGHWAYMEN. HERE ARE
A FEW YOU MAY MEET IN
YOUR TRAVELS.

Reize

This well-intentioned young hero is out to defend the valley, though he does get confused every now and then. His goal is to help people in need, but sometimes he is a little naive.

Reize will hop around the screen while using his twin Crystal Boomerangs to damage you. After you get in a few hits, Reize will cast a spell that creates a shield of spinning fireballs. Dodge his boomerangs and fire, and get in hits when there's an opening.

Reize can be found as an optional encounter on the world map after you defeat Plague Knight, Mole Knight, or Treasure Knight. You can avoid him, but if he is between you and where you want to go, you must confront him.

TRIVIA! REIZE WAS DESIGNED BY DIRECTOR FOR A DAY, DANNY D. HENDERSON

Baz is one big, tough, bad dude with spiky armor and a dangerous whip. As cool as he looks, the Order of No Quarter refused to let him join! Now he is ready to take out his frustrations on anyone who gets in his way.

Baz will run across the screen protected from your Shovel Drops by the whip twirling above his head. When he can he'll try to whip you, but you can dodge him with a well-timed jump. He'll grapple to the hooks above to swing around trying to slam on you from above, the impact of which will emit lightning and stun you if you are on the ground when he lands. If you get stunned, mash the buttons until you are able to recover! When things get tough, Baz will unleash his full might, granting him a lightning burst that shoots lightning diagonally in four directions every few seconds for the rest of the battle.

Baz can be found as an optional encounter on the world map after Shovel Knight leaves the Armor Outpost.

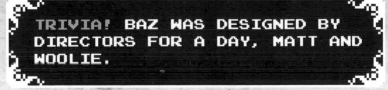

TRIVIA! BAZ WAS DESIGNED BY DIRECTORS FOR A DAY, MATT AND WOOLIE.

Mr. Hat

Mr. Hat's obsession with hats runs deep. Whenever he places a hat on his head, he is granted the powers and abilities of the hat's owner. His skills, strengths, and even his personality can change at the drop of a . . . well, you get the idea.

Mr. Hat's fighting style changes depending on what hat he is wearing. When wearing his military cap, he will toss red-hot iron blades into the air. These will arc down and get stuck in the floor, creating obstacles for you. With his scholar's cap, Mr. Hat will throw tea saucers at you. Be careful to avoid his onslaught. He sips tea, bounces on his cane, and alternates between fancy and military man.

Mr. Hat is found in the Fancy Shop in the Armor Outpost. After you pay off each customer, you'll find yourself alone with Mr. Hat. Only then will he reveal his true intentions!

After you defeat him, you can follow him around the Armor Outpost and talk to him repeatedly. Each time you find him, he will give you gold.

TRIVIA! MR. HAT WAS DESIGNED BY DIRECTOR FOR A DAY, ALEXANDER "HATMAN" HATZIKIDES.

Phantom Striker

Phantom Striker is a warrior shrouded in mystery. He cares for little but perfecting his skill with the foil. He will appear to those he deems worthy of battle and put them to the ultimate test.

When Phantom Striker extends his Foil, it's impossible to hit him from the front, even with the Flare Wand. When he raises his sword, you won't be able to Shovel Drop onto him. Watch out for his lightning attacks. He is testing you. By defeating him with more than half of your health (without using health ichors), he will reward you with more gold.

Phantom Striker can be found as an optional encounter on the world map after you defeat Tinker Knight, Propeller Knight, or Polar Knight.

TRIVIA! PHANTOM STRIKER WAS DESIGNED BY DIRECTOR FOR A DAY, STEVEN NESS.

MANUAL OF MONSTROSITY!!!

BEETO

One of the most common enemies you will face in Shovel Knight. Beeto walks back and forth across platforms. One swipe from your Shovel Blade or a Shovel Drop attack will take care of them.

BIRDER

Birder floats through the air, darting diagonally up and down. Don't let their pulsing colors fool you. You can still slash or Shovel Drop off them, but it's going to take four hits to defeat them.

BLORB

These blob enemies move back and forth slowly and sometimes hop short distances. They won't cause you too much trouble. Warning! Blorbs are flammable and may ignite into dangerous Flaming Blorbs. Don't Shovel Drop on Flaming Blorbs.

WIZZEM

The Wizzem are skilled mages in service of the Enchantress. They charge up their magical attacks and fling them at you. Wizzem come in four varieties: Flare Wizzem, Frost Wizzem, Gear Wizzem, and Lightning Wizzem.

MANTAR

These manta ray-like creatures swim in a back and forth pattern making it easy to avoid them.

GOBCANO

These barnacle creatures spew spores of magma out of their frondy tops. You can slash the spores to send them back to their source, but wouldn't it be better just to avoid these things entirely? Use the anchor against them before you pass under or over them.

TADVOLT

These amphibians were imbued with a lightning aura. Avoid them while they are electrified. Shovel Drop onto them instead when docile.

SERPRIZE

Surprise! Serprize monsters have special skin that allows them to lie in wait, invisible, until they are ready to attack! Some appear in front of you and some appear after you have passed by.

HERMITTACK

Any surface can be crawled along by these crustaceans. Knock one with your Shovel Blade, and it will retreat into its shell, which you can then knock around the room like a bouncy ball. Caution! Metal Hermittacks are immune to the Shovel Blade.

FAIRY

Steer clear of these floating gray enemies, or they'll attack you swiftly with their fangs. Defeat them from a distance, if you can.

RATSPLODER

When these rats are attacked, they'll explode. Run full speed and watch them jump over you, or knock them away and keep your distance. The Flare Wand is useful for triggering their explosion from far away.

GRAPPS

These large tentacles will burst through the walls and floors of the Iron Whale in an attempt to block you. Only the black eye is vulnerable, so attack them there!

MACAWBE

These birds are engulfed in purple flame, but that's not the scary part! They'll hurl bottles of explosive serum at you when they are near. Steer clear of them if you can and avoid the explosions.

HOVERHAFT

Hoverhaft is an enemy with a propeller and a halberd, capable of flight! Attack from a distance with a relic that shoots.

HOVER MEANIE

Green and Blue Hover Meanies operate differently. Blue ones will sometimes provide passive assistance, while green ones will actively try to disrupt you.

INVISISHADE

Invisishades are ghosts that cannot be killed. I mean, come on, they're already dead! Any attack you make will only phase out the Invisishade for a moment before it resumes haunting you. There is a rumor, however, that if you attack the Invisishade with an orb of pure light . . .

GOLDARMOR

These heavily fortified guards are some of the toughest non-boss monsters out there. Their shields will block many of your attacks. Shovel Drop on the Goldarmor's head, and when it raises its shield, land beside it and swipe at it from the side. Goldarmors come in five varieties: Goldarmor, Green Goldarmor, Purple Goldarmor, Silver Goldarmor, Red Goldarmor.

KETTELEG

When you cross a spider and a cauldron you get these sick mutants. Stay clear of the poisonous slime they spew.

BONECLANG

These undead skeletons roam the valley looking for trouble. Some even move without their heads.

BONECLANG HONCHO

These Boneclang bosses wear ornate helmets to show who is in charge. Please note! Boneclang Honcho crowns are very heavy. Use their helmets to weigh things down.

HOPPICLES

Hoppicles use giant horse head shields to protect themselves from scary shovel-wielding knights, but they can still be attacked from behind.

GULPER MAGE

The wicked Gulper Mage summons spinning globes of green energy to throw at unsuspecting knights. You can Shovel Drop on the energy balls.

SLIMULACRA

This doppelgänger is a Plague Knight experiment. Slimulacra will navigate obstacles and even destroy dirt blocks to attack Shovel Knight.

FLOATSOME

These docile jellyfish don't have much interest in Shovel Knight, but they make decent stepping stones. Beware! Blue Floatsome will sometimes electrify themselves.

PLAGUE MINION

They can be quite dangerous if they throw explosive potions at you! They move erratically so get close for an attack.

MOLER

The burrowing Molers are indigenous to the Lost City and love to curl up inside Dig Piles for a long nap. They also have excellent oral hygiene.

CHARFLOUNDER

Be careful not to leap blindly over gaps when Charflounder is around. She'll ambush you with her magma fins. Shovel Drop off her head to get past her.

COGSLOTTER

These workers are builders of machines and specialists of conveyor belts. Watch out for their boomerangs! Try using the Throwing Anchor so you don't have to get too close.

SINE DAGGER

This is what happens when you strap a rocket engine to a knife. The Sine Dagger gets its name from the way it curves up and down as it moves.

BLITZSTEED

The Blitzsteed uses its needle-sharp lance to skewer anyone who gets in the way. The problem with these automated defenders is they never learned how to slow down. They will only charge when you get close to them.

PROPELLER RAT

These rotor-borne rodents use their dangling tails to steer. It's really quite clever if you think about it. Attached to propellers against their will, these docile rodents can be used as stepping stones for those hard-to-reach places.

LIQUID SAMURAI SWORDSMAN

Dark magic is the secret to the Liquid Samurai Swordsman's deception. Royal Guard of the Enchantress, he will try to hide in the ceiling or floor, then materialize and attack you when you get close!

TRIVIA! LIQUID SAMURAI WAS DESIGNED BY MAX VANDUYNE.

LIQUID SAMURAI ARCHER

You'll be facing an arrow ambush when you meet the Liquid Samurai Archer. This warrior uses the same gooey magic as the other liquid samurai, but this one will try to stay away from you and fire arrows from safety. You can knock his arrows back at him from a safe distance!

SPINWULF

Polar Knight trained a pack of Spinwulves to travel with and patrol for him. Try Shovel Dropping onto him or luring him into bottomless pits.

DIVEDRAKE

These drakes will drift through the air up and down or side to side and also dive. Like most flying enemies, they make great stepping stones for your Shovel Drop. Some patrol the skies. Others follow and dive at you.

RUNGSTRIDER

He will hog ladders all day and night, making it impossible to cross his path. Even worse, he throws hammers all the time. Use the Anchor on him to hit from below!

ELECTRODENT

These shockingly dangerous mechanical minions are creations of Tinker Knight. They may look like toys, but don't mess with them! They will charge and dive at you. Even if they look to be defeated, they can reanimate and come at you again.

TUNDREAD

The Tundread are loyal followers of Polar Knight. They even grew bushy white beards to look more like him. Their metal helmets protect them from Shovel Drop attacks. Watch for the pattern of their spear throwing.

FEATS

VICTORY!

Finish the game.

If you read this guide, you already
know how! Never give up!

MUSIC LOVER

Obtain and return all Song Scrolls.

You can get all the Song Scrolls
by following along with this guide.

MASTER ANGLER

Successfully fish five
sparkling fishing spots.

Just watch for sparkling pits!

DECKED OUT

Purchase or unlock all Relics,
Equipment, and Upgrades.

This includes all relics, armors, and Shovel
Blade upgrades. Remember to talk to Chester
under the Village for any relics you missed.

RELIC ROUNDTABLE

Defeat an enemy using each relic.

Don't forget the Fishing Rod!

I SCREAM FOR ICHOR

Sample each of the Trouple King's Ichors.

Ichors are free, so there's not much stopping you from getting this one.

NICE HAT . . .

Help out all the moochers in the Fancy Shop.

Find the moochers in the Armor Outpost. You'll need 3,000 gold to pay them all.

REFLECT LORD

Hit enemies with a reflected projectile thirty times.

Most Wizzems can have their own fireballs reflected back toward them. Try it out!

AGAIN!

Finish New Game Plus, the game mode available after you complete the Shovel Knight quest.

Health is difficult to come by in New Game Plus, but you can fish in any pit (even non-sparkling!) and maybe catch a health restoring fish. Use your ichors wisely!

HALL CHAMPION

Solve the woes of the Hall of Champions.

This should be easy as long as you have the 5,000 gold needed to enter.

WELL MET

Defeat all of the Wandering Travelers.

Most wandering travelers appear on the world map, but don't forget about Mr. Hat in the Armor Outpost!

HALFWAY

Defeat four of the Order of No Quarter.

You'll get this just by progressing on your quest!

HEY BIG SPENDER

Spend a combined 25,000 gold.

Keep spending that hard-earned cash and this feat will be yours in no time.

NO DAMAGE!

Finish any stage without taking damage.

Try this in the Plains of Passage—it's one of the easier stages. Don't forget your Phase Locket!

IMPOSSIBLE!

Finish the game without dying.

This is really tough! The game only saves when you return to the world map, so if you fall in battle, return to the Title Screen without saving and try again.

PENNY PINCHER

Finish the game without spending any money.

Another tough feat— but practice makes perfect.

PERFECT PLATFORMER

Finish the game without falling into a bottomless pit.

If you fall into a pit, you can quit to the Title Screen without saving and try again. You can do this and "Impossible" at the same time.

CHECKPOINTLESS

Destroy every possible checkpoint in the game.

Checkpoints can't be broken in the Plains of Passage. Other than that, you're on your own!

FIRST PURCHASE

Buy your first item.

Just buy any item! Easy-peasy.

MASTER SHOVELER

Purchase all available Shovel Blade upgrades.

Get all 3 of these from the Armor Outpost.

FLARE WANDER

Defeat an enemy with the Flare Wand from more than twenty-five blocks away.

Find an enemy that's at the opposite end of a screen and memorize their location. Then, shoot your Flare Wand from afar and run after the fireball until it hits the enemy.

ANOTHER DIMENSION

Collect 2,000 gold lying on spikes, while using the Phase Locket.

The Forest of Phasing has lots of places with gold on spikes.

SUPER SPHERE

Destroy five enemies within five seconds using Chaos Spheres.

Try this during the dream sequence if you're having trouble. Just throw lots of Spheres!

KNUCKLE DOWN

Hang in the air for more than four seconds using the Dust Knuckles.

You should get this easily by completing Knuckler's Quarry.

REFLECTED RICHES

Bounce the same Alchemy Coin five times in a row.

This can be done on a Goldarmor, but it's even easier with a Bounce Bush!

ARCH OF IRON

Defeat three enemies with one Throwing Anchor.

This is best done in Stranded Ship. Line up 3 Rungstriders and the feat will be yours!

FLYING FEAT

Defeat three enemies using the Propeller Dagger without touching the ground.

Try luring some Propeller Rats into a group, then hit them one after the other.

BOOM!

Defeat five foes at once using the War Horn.

Try doing this during a dream sequence when surrounded by enemies.

CLEARING A PATH

Run over five enemies using
the same Mobile Gear.

Find a straightaway with lots of enemies.
There should be one in the Explodatorium
where you find Chester.

I'M ALIVE!

Finish any stage without dying.

Choose an easier stage to make
this more manageable.

TRUE SHOVELRY

Beat the game without
collecting any relics.

Practice bosses and tough areas without
relics before attempting this. Armors
and shovel upgrades can help!

HURRY UP!

Finish the game
within ninety minutes.

Avoid all optional areas and encounters,
and quit to the Title Screen without
saving if you take too long on a stage.
This one takes lots of practice.

ORDER OF
HOARDERS

Have 50,000 gold on hand.

Break the checkpoints for bonus cash and don't
spend too much. Replay stages to get more
gold if you need it!

GET THE POINT

Destroy all checkpoints
in a single stage.

Choose an easier stage to make
this more manageable.

UNTOUCHED

Emerge unscathed from a battle with any knight of the Order of No Quarter.

Try using the Phase Locket to help you with this! King Knight is your easiest target.

SHOVEL ECONOMY

Finish a level and swing the Shovel Blade fewer than twenty times.

Shovel Dropping and relics don't count, so use those to get you through.

ON A DIET

Finish a level without eating any food.

Avoid food platters and dirt piles in the Plains of Passage.

SPARKER

Finish off any boss using the Ground Spark technique.

You need to be at full health to use the Ground Spark, so keep an ichor handy in case you take damage.

YOU'RE FIRED

Finish off Black Knight with a reflected shot.

Get Black Knight's health down to one bubble. When he charges up his purple fireball attack, get ready to knock it back!

PUNGENT

Listen to all of Croaker's puns.

Find Croaker in the Village, down the ladder. Keep talking to him until you get this. The hardest part is stomaching his humor!

JUGGLER

Impress Mona with your skills.

Get a score of 150 or higher in her minigame.
Remember to jump as you hit the potions to
get the more valuable targets!

DIRT POOR

Don't collect any gold for an
entire Order of No Quarter stage.

This is easiest in Pridemoor Keep.
Take it slowly!

HOOPER

Bounce on the Hoop Kid's
hoop for five seconds.

Try Shovel Dropping on the hoop as close
to the left side of the screen as possible to
have the runway required for this feat.

TROUPPLE ACOLYTE

Discover the secrets of
the Troupple King.

Once you buy a Troupple Chalice,
bring it to the Troupple Pond and marvel
at what you see!

ONLY YOU

Use caution and common sense
around campfires. (That means dig
up the ashes of your campfire.)

Simply dig up the fire pit at your camp
after defeating a boss!

BUT THE ADVENTURE CONTINUES WITH SHOVEL KNIGHT: PLAGUE OF SHADOWS, A WHOLE NEW ADVENTURE STARING PLAGUE KNIGHT! TO UNLOCK IT, FINISH THE GAME! OR ... ENTER THIS SECRET CODE BELOW ON THE TITLE SCREEN. IT CAN BE OUR SECRET!

UNLOCK PLAGUE OF SHADOWS:

(HOLD ATTACK BUTTON) UP, UP, RIGHT, DOWN, LEFT, LEFT (RELEASE ATTACK BUTTON)